A CRY FOR MERCY

Other books by Henri J. M. Nouwen

AGING: THE FULFILLMENT OF LIFE

CLOWNING IN ROME: REFLECTIONS ON SOLITUDE,
CELIBACY, PRAYER AND CONTEMPLATION

CREATIVE MINISTRY

THE GENESEE DIARY: REPORT FROM A TRAPPIST
MONASTERY

IN MEMORIAM

INTIMACY: ESSAYS IN PASTORAL PSYCHOLOGY

THE LIVING REMINDER: PRAYER AND SERVICE IN
MEMORY OF JESUS CHRIST

MAKING ALL THINGS NEW: AN INVITATION TO THE
SPIRITUAL LIFE

OUT OF SOLITUDE: THREE MEDITATIONS ON THE
CHRISTIAN LIFE

REACHING OUT: THREE MOVEMENTS OF THE SPIRITUAL
LIFE

THOMAS MERTON: CONTEMPLATIVE CRITIC

THE WAY OF THE HEART: DESERT SPIRITUALITY AND
CONTEMPORARY MINISTRY

WITH OPEN HANDS

THE WOUNDED HEALER: MINISTRY IN CONTEMPORARY
SOCIETY

A CRY FOR MERCY

Prayers
from the Genesee

BY HENRI J. M. NOUWEN

Illustrations by Earl Thollander

Doubleday & Company, Inc.   Garden City, New York
1981

Library of Congress Cataloging in Publication Data

Nouwen, Henri J. M.
    A cry for mercy.

    1. Prayers. I. Title. II. Title: Prayers from the
Genesee.
    BV245.N69   242'.8
    Library of Congress Catalog Card Number 80–2563
            ISBN: 0-385-17507-8   AACR2
    Text Copyright © 1981 by Henri J. M. Nouwen
Illustrations Copyright © 1981 by Doubleday & Company, Inc.

In Grateful Memory of
Toon Ramselaar

Acknowledgments

This book of prayers would not have been published without the help and encouragement of many people. I would like to thank my friends at the Covenant Peace Community in New Haven and the Sojourners community in Washington, D.C., as well as John Garvey, for their help in selecting, from the many prayers I had written, those prayers that might have meaning for people other than myself. Their suggestions and recommendations were invaluable for the final shape of the text. A sincere word of thanks also goes to Gregory Youngchild and John Mogabgab for their help in the final phrasing of these prayers, and to Robert Moore and Carol Plantinga for typing and retyping the manuscript. As always, I owe a special word of thanks to Phil Zaeder for critically reading the manuscript and making many helpful suggestions. Earl Thollander made the powerful drawings, and Robert Heller and Diana Klemin of Doubleday spent much time and effort working on the form and layout. I am very grateful for their contributions.

Most of all I wish to thank Joseph Núñez for his important role in the making of this book. He made the final selection of the prayers, suggested the chapter divisions, and identified the major movements in the prayers. It was his encouragement that convinced me that the prayers could be published and read by others. I am grateful to him not only for these efforts but also for his friendship and warm support during my last three years at Yale Divinity School.

I dedicate these prayers to the memory of my uncle, Toon Ramselaar, who showed me the way to the priesthood and faithfully supported my work and vocation with his friendship and prayers until his death on January 1, 1981.

Contents

PROLOGUE

From February to August 1979, I lived with the Trappist Monks of the Abbey of the Genesee in upstate New York. It was not the first time I had stayed with them. In 1974 I had been allowed to spend seven months in their monastery, and to share day and night in their life. That first stay had been a very new experience for me. I had never lived in a contemplative monastery, and every day held surprises for me. I had to get used to rising at 2 A.M. and going to bed at 7 P.M. I had to learn how to handle hot pans in the bakery, how to detect small stones in a tub full of raisins, and how to find the right kind of rocks for the new church. But most of all, I had to become familiar with the many hours of prayer and meditation and the many "ins" and "outs" of the common life. Although I never planned to become a Trappist monk, this stay in the monastery was for me like a novitiate. Through the personal guidance of the Abbot, John Eudes Bamberger, these seven months became a time of real spiritual formation. So many things happened both inside and outside of me that I felt a strong need to keep a diary in order to help me sort out the many new experiences. When, after I returned to teaching, I showed my diary notes to my friends, my experiences proved to be much less unique than I had thought. Many could recognize their own struggles in mine. This discovery led me to the decision to publish *The Genesee Diary*.

My second long stay at the Abbey was very different. Instead of being new and surprising, the monastic life was strikingly familiar to me. Everything that had seemed so unusual the first time struck me as quite customary. Nothing had changed. Within a few hours I was back at the hot pans, and on Friday morning Brother Theodore welcomed me at the raisin tub as if I had never left. I needed no instructions or introductions. The same men, the same manners, and the same joyful spirit greeted me. There was nothing dull or boring about this sameness. On the contrary, the familiarity with people, places, and events allowed me to dispense with all the preliminaries and to direct all my attention to the purpose of my stay: to be with God in prayer. The rhythmic sameness of the monastic life revealed to me the sameness of the loving Lord who had been waiting for me to come back and spend some more time with him and him alone. From the moment

I walked into this now so familiar milieu, I realized that there was nothing to keep me there for six months except the Lord himself. There was no longer any need for a diary, no need to record the daily events of the monastic life or the weekly meetings with the Abbot. They had not become unimportant. Rather, they had become as important as breathing and were therefore no longer a subject for daily comments.

The realization that prayer was the only reason to be and to stay at the monastery made me wonder if it might be a good discipline to write at least one prayer a day. At first this thought filled me with many uncertainties. Is my relationship with my Lord not too personal to express on paper? Shouldn't this most sacred form of human expression remain spontaneous and not be constrained by the self-consciousness of writing? Wouldn't writing make prayer more difficult? Although these questions were very real to me, they did not prevent me from following my intuition that it would be worthwhile to sit down at the end of each day and commit to simple words the prayer that was present in my heart at that moment. The result of my discipline is the prayers of which I present a selection in this book. I do this not because they teach anyone how to pray, or because they offer a method of prayer, but because they may point in their awkward powerlessness to the real and very powerful presence of the Divine Spirit who is promised to us by our Lord as a never-failing guide. It is my hope, therefore, that those who recognize in these prayers the cries of their own hearts will also recognize the quiet prayer of God's Spirit in the midst of their own halting and stuttering words.

A year after these prayers were written I added short introductions to suggest some general themes and to indicate certain developments which took place during my six months at the Abbey. I hope that these introductions will make the prayers a little more accessible.

I
February—March: A fearful heart

There is so much fear in us. Fear of people, fear of God and much raw, undefined, free-floating anxiety. I wonder if fear is not our main obstacle to prayer. When we enter into the presence of God and start to sense that huge reservoir of fear in us, we want to run away into the many distractions which our busy world offers us so abundantly. But we should not be afraid of our fears. We can confront them, give words to them and lead them into the presence of him who says: "Do not be afraid, it is I." Our inclination is to show our Lord only what we feel comfortable with. But the more we dare to reveal our whole trembling self to him, the more we will be able to sense that his love, which is perfect love, casts out all our fears.

O Lord Jesus Christ, you who forgave the sins of the paralytic before you let him walk again, I pray that my six months of retreat may make me more aware of your forgiving presence in my life and less concerned about performing well in the eyes of my world. Let me recognize you at that virginal point in the depth of my heart where you dwell and heal me. Let me experience you in that center of my being from which you want to teach and guide me. Let me know you as my loving brother who holds nothing—not even my worst sins—against me, but who wants to touch me in a gentle embrace. Take away the many fears, suspicions, and doubts by which I prevent you from being my Lord, and give me the courage and freedom to appear naked and vulnerable in the light of your presence, confident in your unfathomable mercy.

I know how great my resistance is, how quickly I choose the darkness instead of the light. But I also know that you keep calling me into the light, where I can see not only my sins but your gracious face as well. Be with me every hour of my days in this community, so that I can be for the brothers here a real sign of hope—not because of what I am, but because of what you do in me.

Thank you, O Lord, for bringing me here and giving me another chance to meet you on the road. Praise and glory to you, now and forever. Amen.

Why, O Lord, is it so hard for me to keep my heart directed toward you? Why do the many little things I want to do, and the many people I know, keep crowding my mind, even during the hours that I am totally free to be with you and you alone? Why does my mind wander off in so many directions, and why does my heart desire the things that lead me astray? Are you not enough for me? Do I keep doubting your love and care, your mercy and grace? Do I keep wondering, in the center of my being, whether you will give me all I need if I just keep my eyes on you?

Please accept my distractions, my fatigue, my irritations, and my faithless wanderings. You know me more deeply and fully than I know myself. You love me with a greater love than I can love myself. You even offer me more than I can desire. Look at me, see me in all my misery and inner confusion, and let me sense your presence in the midst of my turmoil. All I can do is show myself to you. Yet, I am afraid to do so. I am afraid that you will reject me. But I know—with the knowledge of faith—that you desire to give me your love. The only thing you ask of me is not to hide from you, not to run away in despair, not to act as if you were a relentless despot.

Take my tired body, my confused mind, and my restless soul into your arms and give me rest, simple quiet rest. Do I ask too much too soon? I should not worry about that. You will let me know. Come, Lord Jesus, come. Amen.

Today, O Lord, I felt intense fear. My whole being seemed to be invaded by fear. No peace, no rest; just plain fear: fear of mental breakdown, fear of living the wrong life, fear of rejection and condemnation, and fear of you. O Lord, why is it so hard to overcome my fear? Why is it so hard to let your love banish my fear? Only when I worked with my hands for a while did it seem that the intensity of the fear decreased.

I feel so powerless to overcome this fear. Maybe it is your way of asking me to experience some solidarity with the fearful people all over the world: those who are hungry and cold in this harsh winter, those who are threatened by unexpected guerrilla attacks, and those who are hidden in prisons, mental institutions, and hospitals. O Lord, this world is full of fear. Make my fear into a prayer for the fearful. Let that prayer lift up the hearts of others. Perhaps then my darkness can become light for others, and my inner pain a source of healing for others.

You, O Lord, have also known fear. You have been deeply troubled; your sweat and tears were the signs of your fear. Make my fear, O Lord, part of yours, so that it will lead me not to darkness but to the light, and will give me a new understanding of the hope of your cross. Amen.

Thank you, O Lord, for this day. I did not feel your presence, I did not hear your voice, I did not see your gentle face, but the raging fear of yesterday was gone, at least for many hours. Thank you for the quiet hours in the bakery, the quiet hours in my room and the quiet hours in church. I could think, read, and pray a little, and I even had a moment in which I could imagine that I might one day feel peace and joy again. Thank you, O Lord, for these good things. I read about "knowing you," about the ways one comes to a knowledge of you, and I pray that what I understand with my mind will descend one day into my heart and give me inner light.

I call to you, O Lord, from my quiet darkness. Show me your mercy and love. Let me see your face, hear your voice, touch the hem of your cloak. I want to love you, be with you, speak to you and simply stand in your presence. But I cannot make it happen. Pressing my eyes against my hands is not praying, and reading about your presence is not living in it.

But there is that moment in which you will come to me, as you did to your fearful disciples, and say, "Do not be afraid; it is I." Let that moment come soon, O Lord. And if you want to delay it, then make me patient. Amen.

Is this going to be a period of purification, Lord? Is this going to be the time when you give me insight into the chains that bind me and the courage to throw them off? Is this going to be my chance to see my prison and escape it?

John Eudes said: "This is a time of purification. A time to identify your ambiguous relationships and your ambivalent attitudes, and to make some decisions and choose some directions." Lord, it is you who said this to me. If I believe in your church and the voice of those who speak in her name, in your name, then it was you who pointed out to me the meaning of my stay here: "Identify and choose."

And you also said, "Pray even when you do not feel attracted to it." Yes, Lord, I will try to pray, even when I am afraid to face you and myself, even when I keep falling asleep or feel as though I am going around in circles, even when it seems that nothing is happening.

Yes, Lord, I will pray—not only with others, not only supported by the rhythms of the choir, but also alone with you. I will try not to be afraid. Lord, give me courage and strength. Let me see myself in the light of your mercy and choose you. Amen.

Wednesday, February 28
Ash Wednesday

O Lord, it is a great grace that I can be in this monastery during Lent. How often have I lived through these weeks without paying much attention to penance, fasting and prayer? How often have I missed the spiritual fruits of this season without even being aware of it? But how can I ever really celebrate Easter without observing Lent? How can I rejoice fully in your resurrection when I have avoided participating in your death?

Yes, Lord, I have to die—with you, through you and in you—and thus become ready to recognize you when you appear to me in your resurrection. There is so much in me that needs to die: false attachments, greed and anger, impatience and stinginess. O Lord, I am self-centered, concerned about myself, my career, my future, my name and fame. Often I even feel that I use you for my own advantage. How preposterous, how sacrilegious, how sad! But yes, Lord, I know it is true. I know that often I have spoken about you, written about you and acted in your name for my own glory and for my own success. Your name has not led me to persecution, oppression, or rejection. Your name has brought me rewards! I see clearly now how little I have died with you, really gone your way and been faithful to it. O Lord, make this Lenten season different from the other ones. Let me find you again. Amen.

Dear Lord, you are the first of the just. You lived the righteous life. It is because of you that your heavenly Father keeps this world in existence and shows his mercy to us sinners. Who am I, Lord, to expect your love, protection, and mercy? Who am I to deserve a place in your heart, in your house, in your kingdom? Who am I, Lord, to hope in your forgiveness, your friendship, your embrace? And still this is what I am waiting for, expecting, even counting on! Not because of my own merits, but solely because of your immense mercy. You lived for us the life that is pleasing to God. O Lord, you are the just one, the blessed one, the beloved one, the righteous one, the gracious one.

I pray that your Father, the Father of all people, the One who created me and sustains me day in and day out, may recognize in me your marks and receive me because of you. Help me to follow you, to unite my life with yours and to become a mirror of your love. Amen.

Monday, March 5

Listen, O Lord, to my prayers. Listen to my desire to be with you, to dwell in your house, and to let my whole being be filled with your presence. But none of this is possible without you. When you are not the one who fills me, I am soon filled with endless thoughts and concerns that divide me and tear me away from you. Even thoughts about you, good spiritual thoughts, can be little more than distractions when you are not their author.

O Lord, thinking about you, being fascinated with theological ideas and discussions, being excited about histories of Christian spirituality and stimulated by thoughts and ideas about prayer and meditation, all of this can be as much an expression of greed as the unruly desire for food, possessions, or power.

Every day I see again that only you can teach me to pray, only you can set my heart at rest, only you can let me dwell in your presence. No book, no idea, no concept or theory will ever bring me close to you unless you yourself are the one who lets these instruments become the way to you.

But, Lord, let me at least remain open to your initiative; let me wait patiently and attentively for that hour when you will come and break through all the walls I have erected. Teach me, O Lord, to pray. Amen.

Wednesday, March 7

O Lord, let me praise you, bless you, worship you. So often my prayer turns into introspective ruminations regarding my own confused feelings and emotions. So often I find myself engaged in reciting a litany of self-complaints, or my attention wanders to people and events that inhabit my restless mind. O Lord, why do I keep focusing so much on what separates me from you? You are the source of all goodness, beauty, and love. You have shown me your mercy by coming to me and lifting me up into your own life through the life of your Church. And still I keep living as if the thousand other things that crowd my mind need more attention than you.

Help me in this struggle to make you the center of my inner life. Give me the grace of prayer. Show me clearly and convincingly how I am fooling myself, and give me the strength to follow this insight. Most of all, O Lord, let me understand that in and through you all my little concerns will be taken care of. You do not despise my worries, but you do ask me to trust that you will deal with them when I simply keep my eyes on you and your kingdom.

Teach me, O Lord, your way. Amen.

Saturday, March 10

O Lord, life passes by swiftly. Events that a few years ago kept me totally preoccupied have now become vague memories; conflicts that a few months ago seemed so crucial in my life now seem futile and hardly worth the energy; inner turmoil that robbed me of my sleep only a few weeks ago has now become a strange emotion of the past; books that filled me with amazement a few days ago now do not seem as important; thoughts which kept my mind captive only a few hours ago, have now lost their power and have been replaced by others.

Why is it so hard to learn from this insight? Why am I continuously trapped by a sense of urgency and emergency? Why do I not see that you are eternal, that your kingdom lasts forever, and that for you a thousand years are like one day? O Lord, let me enter into your presence and there taste the eternal, timeless, everlasting love with which you invite me to let go of my timebound anxieties, fears, preoccupations, and worries. "Seek first the Kingdom," you said, "and all these other things will be given you as well." All that is timebound will show its real meaning when I can look at it from the place where you want me to be, the place of undying love.

Lord, teach me your ways and give me the courage to follow them. Amen.

Sunday, March 11

O Lord, grant me a pure heart so that I can see you and hear you in the splendor of the holy liturgy. How often do I sing the psalms but remain deaf! How often do I see the bread and the wine yet remain blind! O Lord, why do you wait so long to take me to the top of the mountain to show me the light of your transfiguration and to let me listen to the words spoken there? I know, I know. My heart is not pure. I am filled with my own selfish desires, my own ruminations, my own morbid introspection. And so I remain blind and deaf, not seeing and hearing you who desire to be seen and heard. Lord, I really want to see, but my struggle to come to any degree of purity of heart seems so futile. I often feel as if I am surrounded by snares, and that the more I struggle, the more entangled I become. You, O Lord, are the only one who can lead me out of this trap. Take me by the hand and lead me to the top of the mountain. Purify my heart and show me your light.

I do not have to go far. You have given me the words to hear you and the bread and wine to taste you. Come, then, O Lord. I open my senses to your presence. Let me recognize you where you are. Amen.

Monday, March 12

O Lord, who else or what else can I desire but you? You are my Lord, Lord of my heart, mind, and soul. You know me through and through. In and through you everything that is finds its origin and goal. You embrace all that exists and care for it with divine love and compassion. Why, then, do I keep expecting happiness and satisfaction outside of you? Why do I keep relating to you as one of my many relationships, instead of my only relationship, in which all other ones are grounded? Why do I keep looking for popularity, respect from others, success, acclaim, and sensual pleasures? Why, Lord, is it so hard for me to make you the only one? Why do I keep hesitating to surrender myself totally to you?

Help me, O Lord, to let my old self die, to let die the thousand big and small ways in which I am still building up my false self and trying to cling to my false desires. Let me be reborn in you and see through you the world in the right way, so that all my actions, words, and thought can become a hymn of praise to you.

I need your loving grace to travel on this hard road that leads to the death of my old self and to a new life in and for you. I know and trust that this is the road to freedom.

Lord, dispel my mistrust and help me become a trusting friend. Amen.

Saturday, March 17

O Lord Jesus, your words to your Father were born out of your silence. Lead me into this silence, so that my words may be spoken in your name and thus be fruitful. It is so hard to be silent, silent with my mouth, but even more, silent with my heart. There is so much talking going on within me. It seems that I am always involved in inner debates with myself, my friends, my enemies, my supporters, my opponents, my colleagues, and my rivals. But this inner debate reveals how far my heart is from you. If I were simply to rest at your feet and realize that I belong to you and you alone, I would easily stop arguing with all the real and imagined people around me. These arguments show my insecurity, my fear, my apprehensions, and my need for being recognized and receiving attention. You, O Lord, will give me all the attention I need if I would simply stop talking and start listening to you. I know that in the silence of my heart you will speak to me and show me your love. Give me, O Lord, that silence. Let me be patient and grow slowly into this silence in which I can be with you. Amen.

Sunday, March 18

O Lord Jesus Christ, Son of the living God, have mercy on me, a sinner. I am impressed by my own spiritual insights. I probably know more about prayer, meditation, and contemplation than most Christians do. I have read many books about the Christian life, and have even written a few myself. Still, as impressed as I am, I am more impressed by the enormous abyss between my insights and my life.

It seems as if I am standing on one side of a huge canyon and see how I should grow toward you, live in your presence and serve you, but cannot reach the other side of the canyon where you are. I can speak and write, preach and argue about the beauty and goodness of the life I see on the other side, but how, O Lord, can I get there? Sometimes I even have the painful feeling that the clearer the vision, the more aware I am of the depth of the canyon.

Am I doomed to die on the wrong side of the abyss?

Am I destined to excite others to reach the promised land while remaining unable to enter there myself? Sometimes I feel imprisoned by my own insights and "spiritual competence." You alone, Lord, can reach out to me and save me. You alone.

I can only keep trying to be faithful, even though I feel faithless most of the time. What else can I do but keep praying to you, even when I feel dark; to keep writing about you, even when I feel numb; to keep speaking in your name, even when I feel alone. Come, Lord Jesus, come. Have mercy on me, a sinner. Amen.

II
March—April: A cry for mercy

God's mercy is greater than our sins. There is an aware-ness of sin that does not lead to God but to self-pre-occupation. Our temptation is to be so impressed by our sins and failings and so overwhelmed by our lack of generosity that we get stuck in a paralyzing guilt. It is the guilt that says: "I am too sinful to deserve God's mercy." It is the guilt that leads to introspection instead of directing our eyes to God. It is the guilt that has be-come an idol and therefore a form of pride. Lent is the time to break down this idol and to direct our attention to our loving Lord. The question is: "Are we like Judas, who was so overcome by his sin that he could not believe in God's mercy any longer and hanged him-self, or are we like Peter who returned to his Lord with repentance and cried bitterly for his sins?" The season of Lent, during which winter and spring struggle with each other for dominance, helps us in a special way to cry out for God's mercy.

Dear Lord, thank you for the beginning of spring. In the midst of Lent I am made aware that Easter is coming again: the days are becoming longer, the snow is withdrawing, the sun is bringing new warmth, and a bird is singing. Yesterday, during the night prayers, a cat was crying! Indeed, spring announces itself. And tonight, O Lord, I heard you speak to the Samaritan woman. You said: "Anyone who drinks the water that I shall give will never be thirsty again; the water that I shall give will turn into a spring inside him, welling up to eternal life." What words! They are worth many hours, days, and weeks of reflection. I will carry them with me in my preparation for Easter. The water that you give turns into a spring. Therefore, I do not have to be stingy with your gift, O Lord. I can freely let the water come from my center and let anyone who desires drink from it. Perhaps I will even see this spring in myself when others come to it to quench their thirst. So often, Lord, I doubt that there is a spring in me; so often I am afraid that it has dried up or has been filled with sand. But others keep believing in the spring in me even when I do not.

Let the spring of this year and the spring of water in me give me joy, O Lord, my hope and my Redeemer. Amen.

Thursday, March 22

O Lord, your world—the world you loved so much that you wanted to become part of it and experience it to the fullest—is in pain. Small pains and great pains: the pain of my little niece Frederique, who is in the hospital recuperating from surgery on her face; the pain of my father, who travels for the first time without mother and misses her presence deeply; the pain of a monk who feels lonely; the pain of the students who cannot find work . . . But also the pains of the Indians of Mato Grosso who are oppressed, and the pains of the bishop, priests, and sisters who try to be of help; the pains of the many men and women who see the arms race increasing around them and feel discouraged in their attempts to stop it; the pains of the prisoners, the hungry, and the many people who seem happy and content but who feel ripped apart by inner turmoil, guilt feelings, shame, self-doubt, and an inability to overcome their own restlessness.

It is your world, O Lord, that is in pain. You are a compassionate God. You came to share our pains. Please give your people hope, courage, strength, and faith. Let us not be destroyed by the powers of evil which surround us, pervade us and often inhabit us. Drive from us these evil powers, and show us the way to you, who are Light, Life, Truth, Goodness, and, above all, Love. Amen.

O Lord, when shall I die? I do not know and I hope it will not be soon. Not that I feel so attached to this life —I might be much more attached to it than I realize— but I feel so unprepared to face you. I feel that by letting me live a little longer, you reveal your patience, you give me yet another chance to convert myself, you offer me more time to purify my heart. Time is your gift to me.

I remember how I felt ready to die five years ago, when I left the Abbey after a seven-month stay. Now I do not feel that way. I feel restless, not at peace, guilty, doubtful, and very dark. Let my time here be a time of change: a change to inner tranquillity, deep trust in your forgiveness and mercy, and complete surrender to you.

Thank you, Lord, for every day that you give me to come closer to you. Thank you for your patience and goodness. I pray that when I die I will be at peace. Hear my prayer. Amen.

Monday, March 26

O Lord, the great spiritual teacher Isaac of Nineveh said: "He who knows his sins is much greater than he who makes someone rise from the dead. He who can really cry one hour about himself is greater than he who teaches the whole world; he who knows his own weakness is greater than he who sees the angels." These words, O Lord, are so true. I realize that my preoccupation with my sinful deeds is a way of avoiding a confrontation with my real sinfulness. An avoidance of a confrontation with my real sinfulness means also an avoidance of a confrontation with your mercy. As long as I have not experienced your mercy I know that I am still running away from my real sin.

Come, Lord. Break through my compulsions, anxieties, fears, and guilt feelings, and let me see my sin and your mercy. Amen.

O Lord Jesus, you who came to us to show the compassionate love of your Father, make your people know this love with their hearts, minds, and souls. So often we feel lonely, unloved, and lost in this valley of tears. We desire to feel affection, tenderness, care, and compassion, but suffer from inner darkness, emptiness, and numbness. I pray tonight: Come, Lord Jesus, come. Do not just come to our understanding, but enter our hearts—our passions, emotions, and feelings—and reveal your presence to us in our inmost being. As long as you remain absent from that intimate core of our experience, we will keep clinging to people, things, or events to find some warmth, some sense of belonging. Only when you really come, really touch us, set us ablaze with your love, only then will we become free and let go of all false forms of belonging. Without that inner warmth, all our ascetical attempts remain trivial, and we might even get entangled in the complex network of our own good intentions.

O Lord, I pray that your children may come to feel your presence and be immersed in your deep, warm, affective love. And to me, O Lord, your stumbling friend, show your mercy. Amen.

O Lord, this holy season of Lent is passing quickly. I entered into it with fear, but also with great expectations. I hoped for a great breakthrough, a powerful conversion, a real change of heart; I wanted Easter to be a day so full of light that not even a trace of darkness would be left in my soul. But I know that you do not come to your people with thunder and lightning. Even St. Paul and St. Francis journeyed through much darkness before they could see your light. Let me be thankful for your gentle way. I know you are at work. I know you will not leave me alone. I know you are quickening me for Easter—but in a way fitting to my own history and my own temperament.

I pray that these last three weeks, in which you invite me to enter more fully into the mystery of your passion, will bring me a greater desire to follow you on the way that you create for me and to accept the cross that you give to me. Let me die to the desire to choose my own way and select my own cross. You do not want to make me a hero but a servant who loves you.

Be with me tomorrow and in the days to come, and let me experience your gentle presence. Amen.

Friday, March 30

Dear Lord, show me your kindness and your gentleness, you who are meek and humble of heart. So often I say to myself, "The Lord loves me," but very often this truth does not enter into the center of my heart. The fact that I get so easily upset because of a disappointment, so easily angered because of a slight criticism, and so easily depressed because of a slight rejection, shows that your love does not yet fill me. Why, otherwise, would I be so easily thrown off balance? What can people do to me, when I really know that you love me, care for me, protect me, defend me, guide me and support me? What does a small—or even a great—failure mean, when I know that you are with me in all my sorrows and turmoil? Yet time and again I have to confess that I have not let your love descend fully from my mind into my heart, and that I have not let my knowing grow into a real, full knowledge that pervades all of my being.

In the coming weeks, O Lord, I will be able to see again how much you indeed love me. Let these weeks become an opportunity for me to let go of all my resistances to your love and an occasion for you to call me closer to you. Amen.

O Lord, your abundant love became visible today in the abundant beauty of nature. The sun covered the wide fields of the Genesee Valley. The sky was blue with pleasant cloud formations here and there; the trees bare but already suggesting the new season of green leaves; the fields still dark but full of promise. I looked from the ridge out over the valley and was overwhelmed by the stark beauty of the world in which I am living. I was filled with a sense of gratitude, but also with a sense of the shortness of life. When I saw the rich soil, I thought of mother being buried in similar soil only a few months ago, and a strange sadness welled up within the experience of beauty. I can no longer tell her about what I saw, nor can I write her about the new spring, which she always welcomed with much joy. New life, new green leaves, new flowers, new wheat; but this spring she would not call my name and say, "Look here, look there!"

But you, O Lord, say, "The grain of wheat must die to yield a rich harvest." I believe that her death will yield fruits. The day of your resurrection for which I am preparing myself is also a sign that there is hope for all who die. So, let my sadness be a sorrow that makes me more eager to follow you on the way to the cross and beyond it, to that Easter morning with its empty grave.

Let the beauty of the land deepen my joy as well as my sorrow, and thus draw me closer to you, my Lord and my Redeemer. Amen.

Wednesday, April 4

O dear Lord, today I felt the gripping power of my anger. I kept being imprisoned by violent, hostile feelings toward people who had not done for me what they had promised, and in my mind I kept creating angry speeches and vengeful reproaches. Even though I kept trying to direct myself to you, I found no way out of these feelings. I constantly discovered myself back in the center of my rage and could do nothing but present my fury to you. I saw how my rage revealed the degree to which I still belong to this world and its promises and rewards. I even realized that there was no proportion between my inner turmoil and the outer incidents which triggered it. But I could not shake off my anger.

I am humbled before you Lord, aware of how much I depend on your grace to come to the meekness and gentleness of heart that I desire. I feel much calmer now, especially after I wrote down some of my angry feelings. But, Lord, do not test me too often. I want to taste less of my anger and more of your sweetness and love. Give peace to my heart. Amen.

Thursday, April 5

Dear Lord, the unexpected snow today made me think how careful I have to be in making predictions. Just when I had prepared myself for spring and gentler, sunnier weather, winter seemed to return. Aren't you giving me an important warning?

I keep projecting my present condition onto the future. If I feel dark, the future looks dark; if I feel bright, the future looks bright. But who am I to know what life will be like for me tomorrow, next week, next year, or ten years from now? Even more, who am I to know who you will be for me in the year ahead? O Lord, I will not bind you with my own limited and limiting ideas and feelings. You can do so many things with me, things that might seem totally impossible to me. I want at least to remain open to the free movement of your Spirit in my life. Why do I keep saying to myself: "I will never be a saint. I will never be able to overcome my impulses and desires." If I keep saying that, I might prevent you from healing and touching me deeply.

O Lord, let me remain free to let you come whenever and however you desire. Amen.

Monday, April 9

Dear Lord, help me keep my eyes on you. You are the incarnation of Divine Love, you are the expression of God's infinite compassion, you are the visible manifestation of the Father's holiness. You are beauty, goodness, gentleness, forgiveness, and mercy. In you all can be found. Outside of you nothing can be found. Why should I look elsewhere or go elsewhere? You have the words of eternal life, you are food and drink, you are the Way, the Truth, and the Life. You are the light that shines in the darkness, the lamp on the lampstand, the house on the hilltop. You are the perfect Icon of God. In and through you I can see the Heavenly Father, and with you I can find my way to him. O Holy One, Beautiful One, Glorious One, be my Lord, my Savior, my Redeemer, my Guide, my Consoler, my Comforter, my Hope, my Joy and my Peace. To you I want to give all that I am. Let me be generous, not stingy or hesitant. Let me give you all—all I have, think, do and feel. It is yours, O Lord. Please accept it and make it fully your own. Amen.

Tuesday, April 10

Dear Lord, your disciple Peter wanted to know who would betray you. You pointed to Judas but a little later also to him. Judas betrayed, Peter denied you. Judas hanged himself, Peter became the apostle whom you made the first among equals. Lord, give me faith, faith in your endless mercy, your boundless forgiveness, your unfathomable goodness. Let me not be tempted to think that my sins are too great to be forgiven, too abominable to be touched by your mercy. Let me never run away from you but return to you again and again, asking you to be my Lord, my Shepherd, my Stronghold, and my Refuge. Take me under your wing, O Lord, and let me know that you do not reject me as long as I keep asking you to forgive me. Perhaps my doubt in your forgiveness is a greater sin than the sins I consider too great to be forgiven. Perhaps I make myself too important, too great when I think that I cannot be embraced by you anymore. Lord, look at me, accept my prayer as you accepted Peter's prayer, and let me not run away from you in the night as Judas did.

Bless me, Lord, in this Holy Week, and give me the grace to know your loving presence more intimately. Amen.

Friday, April 13
Good Friday

O dear Lord, what can I say to you on this holy night? Is there any word that could come from my mouth, any thought, any sentence? You died for me, you gave all for my sins, you not only became man for me but also suffered the most cruel death for me. Is there any response? I wish that I could find a fitting response, but in contemplating your Holy Passion and Death I can only confess humbly to you that the immensity of your divine love makes any response seem totally inadequate. Let me just stand and look at you. Your body is broken, your head wounded, your hands and feet are split open by nails, your side is pierced. Your dead body now rests in the arms of your Mother. It is all over now. It is finished. It is fulfilled. It is accomplished. Sweet Lord, gracious Lord, generous Lord, forgiving Lord, I adore you, I praise you, I thank you. You have made all things new through your passion and death. Your cross has been planted in this world as the new sign of hope.

Let me always live under your cross, O Lord, and proclaim the hope of your cross unceasingly. Amen.

III
April—May: Rays of hope

The Easter season is a time of hope. There still is fear, there still is a painful awareness of sinfulness, but there also is light breaking through. Something new is happening, something that goes beyond the changing moods of our life. We can be joyful or sad, optimistic or pessimistic, tranquil or angry, but the solid stream of God's presence moves deeper than the small waves of our minds and hearts. Easter brings the awareness that God is present even when his presence is not directly noticed. Easter brings the good news that, although things seem to get worse in the world, the Evil One has already been overcome. Easter allows us to affirm that although God seems very distant and although we remain preoccupied with many little things, our Lord walks with us on the road and keeps explaining the Scriptures to us. Thus there are many rays of hope casting their light on our way through life.

Sunday, April 15
Easter Sunday

Dear Lord, risen Lord, light of the world, to you be all praise and glory! This day, so full of your presence, your joy, your peace, is indeed your day.

I just returned from a walk through the dark woods. It was cool and windy, but everything spoke of you. Everything: the clouds, the trees, the wet grass, the valley with its distant lights, the sound of the wind. They all spoke of your resurrection; they all made me aware that everything is indeed good. In you all is created good, and by you all creation is renewed and brought to an even greater glory than it possessed at its beginning.

As I walked through the dark woods at the end of this day, full of intimate joy, I heard you call Mary Magdalene by her name and heard how you called from the shore of the lake to your friends to throw out their nets. I also saw you entering the closed room where your disciples were gathered in fear. I saw you appearing on the mountain and at the outskirts of the village. How intimate these events really are. They are like special favors to dear friends. They were not done to impress or overwhelm anyone, but simply to show that your love is stronger than death.

O Lord, I know now that it is in silence, in a quiet moment, in a forgotten corner that you will meet me, call me by name and speak to me a word of peace. It is in my stillest hour that you become the risen Lord to me.

Dear Lord, I am so grateful for all you have given me this past week. Stay with me in the days to come.

Bless all who suffer in this world and bring peace to your people, whom you loved so much that you gave your life for them. Amen.

Monday, April 16

Dear Lord, the women who saw the angel at the empty tomb came away with awe and joy. Yet, at the same time, they experienced fear. I have felt this myself today. I am filled with joy during these Easter days, but I still feel fear, apprehension, and distance. O Lord, I wonder if I would recognize you as did Mary Magdalene, the disciples, and the travelers to Emmaus. Is my heart able to recognize you? Have I really given you all my attention while you spoke with me during the years? Do I have eyes that can see and ears that can hear? Please, Lord, do not pass me by, do not ignore me. Show me your loving face and let me hear your consoling voice; all will be different. Do not let me be so busy with the affairs of the world that I do not even notice that something is happening that is really real!

Come, Lord, show me your face and lead me always closer to you. Amen.

Thursday, April 19

Dear Lord, after your resurrection you opened the minds of your disciples to understand the Scriptures. You made it clear to them that Moses, the prophets, and the psalmist had spoken about you. You revealed to them the great mystery that it was ordained that you should suffer and so enter into your glory.

Tonight I pray to you for an always deeper understanding of the Scriptures and an always greater awareness that you are in the center, or—to say it with the words of Vincent van Gogh—that your Gospel is the top of the mountain of which the Old Testament and the letters of the Apostles are the slopes. Let me see your presence in the psalms, in the prophets and in the great story of the people of Israel, and let this insight help me better understand my own history, my own struggle and my own pain.

Please, Lord, join me on the road, enter into my closed room, and take my foolishness away. Open my mind and heart to the great mystery of your active presence in my life, and give me the courage to help others discover your presence in their lives.

Thank you, Lord, for this day. Amen.

Friday, April 20

Dear Lord, I have been thinking today about that mysterious meeting that your disciples had with you on the shore of the Lake of Tiberias. They had breakfast with you. You, in fact, invited them. You "stepped forward, took the bread and gave it to them, and the same with the fish."

I pause at this mysterious meeting. I feel drawn by the closeness, yet I also sense a distance; I realize that there is a familiarity, but I also know that there is a certain reserve; I am touched by the joy but I also am moved by the deep awe; I recognize your presence, but I also experience that you are still absent. I can truly understand that none of your disciples was bold enough to ask: "Who are you?"

Lord, you are making me understand that while you reveal yourself to me you also hide from me, that while you invite me to eat with you you also ask me not to touch you. Often I feel this tension in me and want it to disappear. I desire no distance, no fear, no apprehension. But who am I to be so bold as even to ask for such a thing? Let me be grateful, Lord, that you call me, a sinner, and give me bread and fish. I am not ready to see your splendor. I would die. You hide yourself so that I may live and be purified. Thank you, O Lord. Amen.

Sunday, April 22

Dear Lord, this afternoon I shared my feelings of guilt and sinfulness with one of the monks. He gave me good advice. He kept urging me to move away continually from introspection and self-preoccupation and to concentrate on expressing my love for you.

What most helped me was his remark that nothing more terrible could happen than what had already happened: your death, O Lord, which is the most terrible, sinful, and frightful event in the whole of history. We human beings killed you, our brother, Son of the Most High. Whatever will happen—hunger, oppression, or war—can never be worse than what has already taken place. But you overcame the worst. You did not reject us, but made your death the sign of our redemption. Your love became fully visible to us in and through your death. Whatever evil I did or will do, you have already suffered it and showed me that it is never so evil that I cannot return to you. O dear Lord, let me never doubt your forgiveness, but let me always remember that you died for my sins and rose from the dead as a sign of your forgiving love. Let not my guilt, but your love, guide me. Amen.

Sunday, April 29

Dear Lord, give me a growing desire to pray. It remains so hard for me to give my time generously to you. I am still greedy for time—time to be useful, effective, successful, time to perform, excel, produce. But you, O Lord, ask nothing else than my simple presence, my humble recognition of my nakedness, my defenseless confession of my sins, so that you can let the rays of your love enter my heart and give me the deep knowledge that I can love because you have loved me first, that I can offer acceptance because you have accepted me first, and that I can do good because you have shown me your goodness first.

What holds me back? What makes me so hesitant and stingy, so careful and calculating? Do I still doubt that I need nothing besides you? Do I still want to build up some kind of reserve in case you might not come through? Please, Lord, help me to give up these immature games, and let me love you freely, boldly, courageously, and generously. Amen.

Monday, April 30

Dear Lord, although life in this monastery is quiet and peaceful—with the days passing by in a joyful liturgical rhythm and life together in harmony and brotherly love —most people experience this time as an apocalyptic time full of dangers and threats. The chance of a nuclear war is real, hunger is increasing in many parts of the world, violence and hatred cover the front pages of the daily newspapers, and millions of people wonder how they are going to make it through another year, week, or even day.

I pray tonight for all who witness for you in this world: ministers, priests, and bishops, men and women who have dedicated their lives to you, and all those who try to bring the light of the Gospel into the darkness of this age. Give them courage, strength, perseverance, and hope; fill their hearts and minds with the knowledge of your presence, and let them experience your name as their refuge from all dangers. Most of all, give them the joy of your Spirit, so that wherever they go and whomever they meet they will remove the veil of depression, fatalism, and defeatism and will bring new life to the many who live in constant fear of death. Lord, be with all who bring the Good News. Amen.

Dear Lord, you once said, "The will of him who sent me is that I should lose nothing of all that he has given to me." These words are a source of consolation this day. They show that you are doing all that can be done to keep me in your love. They demonstrate that indeed you entered this world to save me, to free me from the bonds of evil and sin, and to lead me to your Father's house. They reveal that you are willing to struggle against the strong powers which pull me away from you. Lord, you want to keep me, hold onto me, fight for me, protect me, help me, support me, comfort me, and present me to your Father. It indeed is your divine task not to lose me! And yet I am free. I can separate myself from you, and you will never take this freedom away from me. Oh, what a wonder of love, what a mystery of divine grace! Please, Lord, let me freely choose for your love so that I will not be lost to you. Amen.

Thursday, May 3

Dear Lord, your apostle Philip joined an Ethiopian pilgrim returning from Jerusalem to his country. As you did when you joined the men going to Emmaus, so your apostle explained the Scriptures to this pilgrim and made it clear that they were speaking about you. I pray that this will be my ministry: to join people on their journey and to open their eyes to see you. Many people are searching. Often they are studying, reading, discussing, writing, and performing to find an answer to their most intimate questions. But many remain groping in the dark. Give me the courage to join them and say to them as Philip did, "Do you understand what you are reading?" Give me the intelligence and conviction to speak to them about you, who are the Way, the Truth and the Life. Give me the discernment to know when they are ready to be baptized by water and the Holy Spirit.

But, please, Lord, also give me the encouragement you gave to Philip when you said to him, "Go up and meet that chariot." You know that I am shy and fearful. Let me be confident and free. Amen.

Wednesday, May 9

Dear Lord, free me from my dark past, into which I often feel myself falling as if into a deep cistern. You are the light that has come into the world so that whoever believes in you need not stay in darkness any longer. Do not allow me to sink back into my own dark pit, O Lord, but let your warm, gentle, life-giving light lift me from my grave. Vincent van Gogh painted you as the sun when he painted the resurrection of Lazarus. In so doing, he wanted to express his own liberation from a dark, imprisoning past. Lord, keep showing me your light, and give me the strength to rise and follow you without ever looking back. You are my Strength, my Refuge, and my Stronghold. As long as I keep my eyes on you, there is no reason to return to past events, past patterns, past ideas. In your light all becomes new. Let me be fully yours. Amen.

Dear Lord, in the midst of much inner turmoil and restlessness, there is a consoling thought: maybe you are working in me in a way I cannot yet feel, experience or understand. My mind is not able to concentrate on you, my heart is not able to remain centered, and it seems as if you are absent and have left me alone. But in faith I cling to you. I believe that your Spirit reaches deeper and further than my mind or heart, and that profound movements are not the first to be noticed.

Therefore, Lord, I promise I will not run away, not give up, not stop praying, even when it all seems useless, pointless, and a waste of time and effort. I want to let you know that I love you even though I do not feel loved by you, and that I hope in you even though I often experience despair. Let this be a little dying I can do with you and for you as a way of experiencing some solidarity with the millions in this world who suffer far more than I do. Amen.

Sunday, May 13

Dear Lord, I bring before you all the people who experience failure in their search for a creative, affectionate relationship. Many single people feel lonely and unable to sustain a friendship for a long period of time; many married people feel frustrated in their marriage and separate to go different ways; many children cannot speak to their parents; and many parents have become afraid of their children. All around me I see the hunger for love and the inability to experience it in a deep and lasting way.

O Lord, look with favor on us, your people, and impart your love to us—not as an idea or concept, but as a lived experience. We can only love each other because you have loved us first. Let us know that first love so that we can see all human love as a reflection of a greater love, a love without conditions and limitations.

Heal those who feel hurt in their most intimate self, who feel rejected, misunderstood, or even misused.

Show them your healing love and help them on the way to forgiveness and reconciliation. Amen.

IV
May—June: The power
of the Spirit

The Holy Spirit whom Jesus promised to his followers is the great gift of God. Without the Spirit of Jesus we can do nothing, but in and through his Spirit we can live free, joyful, and courageous lives. We cannot pray, but the Spirit of Christ can pray in us. We cannot create peace and joy, but the Spirit of Christ can fill us with a peace and joy which is not of this world. We cannot break through the many barriers which divide races, sexes, and nations, but the Spirit of Christ unites all people in the all-embracing love of God. The Spirit of Christ burns away our many fears and anxieties and sets us free to move wherever we are sent. That is the great liberation of Pentecost.

Dear Lord, teach me the way to poverty. It is so clear that possessions lead to many false worries and that these worries prevent me from paying attention to you. You are with me all the time, you want to speak to me, you want to guide me, teach me, counsel me, and you want to show me where to go. I know that you stand at the door and knock. But I am so busy with other things, that I cannot hear you; so preoccupied with what to read, what to write, what to say, or what to do, that I do not realize that all those problems would not exist if I listened to you and stopped listening to my own inner turmoil. Help me, Lord, to become poor, in all the meanings of that word. Show me how to use the money that comes my way, show me how to use the knowledge I have acquired, show me how to use the relationships, and contacts that have become part of my life. Let all this not prevent me from following you but rather become a way to serve you and your kingdom. Let me become free from all my false worries and concerns, and live with a poor and free heart so that you alone are my Lord. Amen.

Saturday, May 19

Dear Lord, help me to be strong and faithful when the day comes for me to learn that the world hates you and those who believe in you. The friendship and intimacy you offer me does not belong to this world. It is not based on competition, rivalry, success, jealousy, and suspicion. It is not acquired by manipulation or extortion. Your love and goodness are free gifts coming from the abundance of your heart. Your peace and joy are like streams flowing freely from your innermost self to your people. But the world in which I live has other ways and other rules, and it responds to you and your abundant love with hatred and persecution.

I do not know if I am ready for that. I am weak, fearful, and easily in doubt. But I trust that you will be at my side and will give me the words when the hour comes to witness for your love. As for now, O Lord, deepen my knowledge of your love. Amen.

Thursday, May 24
Feast of the Ascension

Dear Lord, at the end of this Ascension Day I am filled with gratitude. I realize that on this day you concluded your stay among us and the great mystery of your incarnation became visible in its fullness. Your earthly life, which began with Gabriel's visit to your Mother, was concluded when you were lifted up in a cloud and taken from the sight of your disciples. You, O Lord, Son of God, Son of Man, Emmanuel, Messiah, Redeemer of all people, you indeed shared with us all that is human and led our humanity to the right hand of your Heavenly Father. When you were no longer seen by your friends and had left them behind, you had fulfilled your divine mission. You taught us all we need to know; you did all that could be done; you gave us all that you had.

What would my life have been without knowing you? All my joys and pains are connected with your having come into this world.

Thank you, Lord, for your life on this earth and for calling me to tell the story of your life to all people. Amen.

Friday, May 25

Dear Lord, even when I know everything about you, even when I have studied all the Scriptures with care, even when I have a great desire and willpower to work in your service, I can do nothing without the gift of your Spirit. Often I realize that the clearest vision of the true life, and the most sincere wish to live it, is not enough to make me a true disciple. Only when your Spirit has entered into the depth of my being can I be a real Christian, a man who lives in and with and through you.

You made it clear to your friends that they should not leave Jerusalem but should "stay in the city until they are clothed with the power from on high."

O Lord, I pray for the power of your Spirit. Let this power invade me and transform me into a real disciple, willing to follow you even where I would rather not go. Amen.

Dear Lord, you came to this world not only as a man, but specifically as a Jewish man. I will never fully understand your words, your gestures, your actions unless I fully realize your Jewishness. It is becoming clearer to me every day that the Jews have much to teach me not only about the Old Testament and the Jewish religion, but also about you. Lord, I pray for the Jews. Give them peace and freedom after the many centuries of persecution and oppression; give them a safe home in Israel where they can come and go, dwell and work without fear; give them a deep love for their own history and tradition; give their children the "Shalom" in its full sense of physical, mental, and spiritual well-being. I pray especially that you give to the Jews the generosity of heart to keep forgiving us Christians for the cruelties and atrocities to which we have subjected them and their forefathers and foremothers.

Finally I pray that the Jews will see you more and

more as one of their own: a brother, a rabbi, a teacher who honored and respected the Jewish law and who spoke in the tradition of the great prophets.

O Lord, deepen my love for your people. Amen.

Monday, May 28
Memorial Day

Dear Lord, awaken the people of the earth and their leaders to the realization of the madness of the nuclear arms race. Today we mourn the dead of past wars, but will there be anyone to mourn the dead of the next one? O Lord, turn us away from our foolish race to self-destruction; let us see that more and more weaponry indeed means more of a chance to use it. Please, Lord, let the great talents you have given to your creatures not fall into the hands of the powers and principalities for whom death is the means as well as the goal. Let us see that the resources hidden in your earth are for feeding each other, healing each other, offering shelter to each other, making this world a place where men, women and children of all races and nations can live together in peace.

Give us new prophets who can speak openly, directly, convincingly and lovingly to kings, presidents, senators, church leaders, and all men and women of good will, prophets who can make us wage peace instead of war. Lord, make haste to help us. Do not come too late! Amen.

Thursday, May 31
Feast of the Visitation

Dear Lord, the words spoken between Elizabeth and your holy Mother are so rich, deep, and beautiful that I find it hard to decide which word to dwell upon.

But it is important to keep realizing that Elizabeth did not call your Mother "blessed" because of her purity, her wisdom, or her beauty but because of her faith in the promise given to her.

"The Holy Spirit will come upon you and the power of the Most High will cover you with its shadow." The promise given to your Mother became the promise given to your disciples when you left them, and it is the promise that is giving me hope these days.

Give me the faith of your Mother and let your promise be fulfilled in me. Send your Holy Spirit and may you, through your Spirit, find a dwelling place in me. Amen.

Saturday, June 2

Dear Lord, let your Spirit give me the power to overcome all hesitation, to take away all fear, and to remove
all shyness. May your Spirit help me respond gratefully
to you, speak freely about you to everyone I meet, and
act courageously to let your kingdom come. You, Lord,
not only gave me a baptism in water but also a baptism
in the Holy Spirit. Let that baptism in your Spirit become visible in my life. Let it allow me to experience
your presence not only through the darkness of faith
but also through new sensitivities that allow me to see,
hear, taste, touch and even smell a reality that reaches
beyond what my natural senses perceive. Let your
Spirit bring reconciliation, joy, peace, gentleness, and
generosity into the hearts of those with whom I live
and for whom I work. But most of all, O Lord, let your
Spirit fill me with love so that all I think, say and do
will be done out of love for you who lived, died, and
rose from the dead for my sake. Amen.

Sunday, June 3
Feast of Pentecost

Dear Lord, when your Spirit descended upon your disciples, they spoke the languages of those who came to hear their witness. Tonight I pray that in our time your Spirit will also break through the many barriers that divide nations and people. Let there be unity among us who inhabit this world. Give us the strength to transcend our physical, emotional, and psychological differences and recognize that it is your Holy Spirit who unites us by making us all participants in your own divine life. Let your Spirit open our eyes and ears to your ongoing presence among us. Let us recognize you when we serve each other, work together for reconciliation and peace, and unite our talents to build a better world. Without your Spirit we are powerless, but with and in your Spirit we can renew the world. Do not leave us alone, but let your Spirit enter into our hearts so that together we can prepare the day of your glorious return and can praise you, thank you, honor you, and love you all the days of our lives. Amen.

Monday, June 4

_____

Dear Lord, I pray that you will let your Spirit do his restoring work in me, even though I myself do not experience his presence directly. I would like to suddenly feel a strong wind, to see fiery tongues, to speak foreign languages, and to be so full of your Spirit that I could do nothing but announce the Good News to all who want to hear me. But this expresses more impatience than faith, more desire for the spectacular than quiet hope, more impulsiveness than deep and persistent love. You *are* sending your Spirit, Lord, I know. Even after a few months here I have sensed your work in my soul, a very quiet ongoing work. My experiences of darkness, guilt, and despair have lost their intensity, my moments of restlessness and fatigue occur less frequently, and in the midst of all my distractions I notice that my inner eye turns to you more easily than before. No dramatic changes are present, but yet I am aware of movements far beyond my own comprehension.

I thank you, Lord, for the gift of your Spirit. May

the weeks to come strengthen and deepen his presence in me. Amen.

V
June—July: The needs
of the world

The Spirit of Christ sends us into the world. To the degree that we are guided not by our fears but by the power of the Spirit, we become aware of the needs of the world and we experience a deep desire to be of service. The prisoners, the sick, the hungry, the homeless, as well as the many who are entangled in war or in the preparation for war, are shown to us as brothers and sisters with whom we are united in solidarity.

Tuesday, June 12

Dear Lord, it does not take much for me to forget you. The world, my world, has so many ways of demanding my attention that I quickly allow myself to be turned away from you. You are present in this world, in my life, in all that happens. But your presence is quiet, gentle, and unspectacular. Silence, solitude, quiet prayer, a peaceful conversation, and reflective reading help me recognize that you are with me, that you call me, that you challenge me and, most of all, that you invite me into your house of peace and joy. Yet the loud voices of the world, the endless variety of "musts" and "oughts" and the illusion that everything has the quality of an emergency, all these things pull me away from the place where you dwell and make me live as if I and not you have to save the world.

A few days away from this house of prayer has made it very clear how easily I am seduced into thinking that everything except you is worth time, attention, and effort. Lord, I pray tonight that you deepen and strengthen my awareness of your presence so that I can live in the world without being of it. Let the last two months of my stay in this monastery make my encounter with you as strong and deep and lasting as that of Saul on the road to Damascus, so that I can see the world with the new sight you are giving me. Amen.

Wednesday, June 13

Dear Lord, you are the Truth. When I keep myself rooted in you, I will live in the Truth. Help me, Lord, to live a truthful life, a life in which I am guided not by popularity, public opinion, current fashion, or convenient formulations but by a knowledge that comes from knowing you.

There may be times during which holding onto the Truth is hard and painful, and leads to oppression, persecution, and death. Be with me, Lord, if that time ever comes. Let me then experience that to hold onto the Truth means to hold onto you, that Love and Truth can never be separated, and that to live truthfully is the same as being faithful to a loving relationship.

Lord, bring me always closer to you who are my teacher, always teaching me out of love. Amen.

Sunday, June 17
Feast of Corpus Christi

Dear Lord, on this day dedicated to the Eucharist, I think of the thousands of people suffering from lack of food and of the millions suffering from lack of love. While I am well fed and well cared for, while I am enjoying the fruits of the earth and the love of the brothers, I am aware of the physical and emotional destitution of so many of my fellow human beings.

Isn't my faith in your presence in the breaking of the bread meant to reach out beyond the small circle of my brothers to the larger circle of humanity and to alleviate suffering as much as possible?

If I can recognize you in the Sacrament of the Eucharist, I must also be able to recognize you in the many hungry men, women, and children. If I cannot translate my faith in your presence under the appearance of bread and wine into action for the world, I am still an unbeliever.

I pray therefore, Lord, deepen my faith in your Eucharistic presence and help me find ways to let this faith bear fruit in the lives of many. Amen.

Friday, June 22

Dear Lord, when your side was pierced, and water and blood came forth, the church was born; a new community founded on baptism and the sacrificial breaking of the bread. It is your love, manifested on the cross, that gave birth to a new life, a new way of living, a new fellowship, a new message.

O Lord, I pray that your Church as a community of love born on your cross will withstand the powers that are threatening us with division and destruction. Make the love of your church strong enough to dismantle the nuclear warheads, missiles, and submarines and bring sanity to those who keep making more and more of them day after day. Give your people insight, courage and faith to take a stand against this madness, in which defense becomes the same as mutual annihilation.

O Lord, let our love be strong and fearless, and let your name be spoken as a sign of hope. Amen.

Dear Lord, thousands of people are driven from their countries; thousands are dying at sea in boats, unable to find a welcome port; thousands are kept in camps without much hope for a normal family life in the future. Day after day the number of refugees increases, and day after day it becomes clear that we are living in a very inhospitable world.

O Lord, show me ways to respond to this human tragedy. Show me how I can live in fidelity to your word in these days of anguish and despair for countless people. Give me an enlightened mind, a fervent heart, and a strong will so that I can speak and act according to your great commandment of love.

I know what is happening, I realize the emergency of the situation, and I am convinced of the need to make a generous response. But I do not yet know clearly what you ask me to do here and now. I pray that you will help me to find my way of being your disciple. Amen.

Thursday, June 28

O Lord, you came to bring peace, to offer reconciliation, to heal the separation between people, and to
show how it is possible for men and women to overcome their differences and to celebrate their unity. You
revealed your Father as a Father of all people, a Father
without resentments or desires for revenge, a Father
who cares for each one of his children with an infinite
love and mercy and who does not hesitate to invite
them into his own house.

But our world today does not look like a world that
knows your Father. Our nations are torn by chaos,
hatred, violence, and war. In many places death rules.
El Salvador, Northern Ireland, Iran, and many other
countries have not experienced peace for many years.
Even in countries which are officially at peace, such as
Spain, Italy, and Turkey, violence is never absent. And
our own country, is it not more warlike than peaceful?

O Lord, do not forget the world into which you

came to save your people; do not turn your back on your children who desire to live in harmony but who are constantly entangled in fear, anger, lust, violence, greed, suspicion, jealousy and hunger for power. Bring your peace to this world, a peace we cannot make ourselves. Awaken the consciousness of all peoples and their leaders; raise up men and women full of love and generosity who can speak and act for peace, and show us new ways in which hatred can be left behind, wounds can be healed, and unity can be restored.

O God, come to our assistance. O Lord, make haste to help us. Amen.

Friday, June 29
Feast of Peter and Paul

Dear Lord, you certainly chose vibrant, intense, passionate men to spread your word! Peter, impulsive, active, energetic, and very exuberant; Paul, sharp, committed, and possessing unusual stamina. These two men were to be the founders of the young communities of Christians spread out from Jerusalem to Rome.

Peter denied you; Paul persecuted your followers; but with the passion with which they first said "No," they also said "Yes" after they had seen your face and heard your call.

You, O Lord, did not choose the lukewarm, the neutral, or the middle-of-the-road type. You called very outspoken people, able to experience ecstasy as well as depression.

I thank you, Lord, for giving me this comforting understanding. Let me have the courage to live fully even when it is risky, vibrantly even when it leads to pain, and spontaneously even when it leads to mistakes. But let me live always for you, so that I can be molded by you into an instrument of your word. Amen.

Sunday, July 1

Dear Lord, by the power that went out from you a woman was healed of an illness no doctor had been able to cure and a young girl was called to life. You revealed that God is the God of life, in whom no death can be found.

O Lord, I pray, touch our death-oriented world and call forth new life. Bring life, joy, and new vitality to those who are walking in the shadow of death, to those who are ill and dying, to those who are depressed and in despair, to those who are resentful and violent. Wherever I look in this world, I see the power of death at work. I see it in the conflicts between nations as well as in the rivalries between people. Do not let your people be conquered by these dark forces, but let your life-giving power enter their bodies, hearts and minds, and let them recognize you as the Son of the God who is not a God of the dead but of the living. Amen.

Tuesday, July 3

Dear Lord, your apostle Thomas wanted to see you and touch your wounds. He was not satisfied with the enthusiastic words of his friends. He wanted to experience your presence with his own senses.

How I can understand that desire! Haven't I been praying to you often and fervently to let me see you and touch you? And what do you say? "Blessed are those who have not seen and yet believe."

Are you asking me to stay in the darkness of faith and surrender to you that feverish and impatient desire for a direct, sensible experience? Are you inviting me to live my life in simple faith, obedient to the witnesses who saw you after your death and who based their teaching on the fact that they indeed saw you alive?

O Lord, I believe; help my unbelief. Amen.

Saturday, July 7

Dear Lord, today I thought of the words of Vincent van Gogh: "It is true there is an ebb and flow, but the sea remains the sea." You are the sea. Although I experience many ups and downs in my emotions and often feel great shifts and changes in my inner life, you remain the same. Your sameness is not the sameness of a rock, but the sameness of a faithful lover. Out of your love I came to life; by your love I am sustained; and to your love I am always called back. There are days of sadness and days of joy; there are feelings of guilt and feelings of gratitude; there are moments of failure and moments of success; but all of them are embraced by your unwavering love.

My only real temptation is to doubt in your love, to think of myself as beyond the reach of your love, to remove myself from the healing radiance of your love. To do these things is to move into the darkness of despair.

O Lord, sea of love and goodness, let me not fear too much the storms and winds of my daily life, and let me know that there is ebb and flow but that the sea remains the sea. Amen.

VI
July—August: A grateful heart

Fear and anxiety never totally leave us. But slowly they lose their domination as a deeper and more central experience begins to present itself. It is the experience of gratitude. Gratitude is the awareness that life in all its manifestations is a gift for which we want to give thanks. The closer we come to God in prayer, the more we become aware of the abundance of God's gifts to us. We may even discover the presence of these gifts in the midst of our pains and sorrows. The mystery of the spiritual life is that many of the events, people, and situations that for a long time seemed to inhibit our way to God become ways of our being united more deeply with him. What seemed a hindrance proves to be a gift. Thus gratitude becomes a quality of our hearts that allows us to live joyfully and peacefully even though our struggles continue.

Tuesday, July 10

Dear Lord, I will remain restless, tense, and dissatisfied until I can be totally at peace in your house. But I am still on the road, still journeying, still tired and weary, and still wondering if I will ever make it to the city on the hill. With Vincent van Gogh, I keep asking your angel, whom I meet on the road, "Does the road go uphill then all the way?" And the answer is, "Yes to the very end." And I ask again: "And will the journey take all day long?" And the answer is: "From morning till night, my friend."

So I go on, Lord, tired, often frustrated, irritated, but always hopeful to reach one day the eternal city far away, resplendent in the evening sun.

There is no certainty that my life will be any easier in the years ahead, or that my heart will be any calmer. But there is the certainty that you are waiting for me and will welcome me home when I have persevered in my long journey to your house.

O Lord, give me courage, hope, and confidence. Amen.

.

Friday, July 13

Dear Lord, you have sent me into this world to preach your word. So often the problems of the world seem so complex and intricate that your word strikes me as embarrassingly simple. Many times I feel tongue-tied in the company of people who are dealing with the world's social and economic problems.

But you, O Lord, said, "Be clever as serpents and innocent as doves." Let me retain innocence and simplicity in the midst of this complex world. I realize that I have to be informed, that I have to study the many aspects of the problems facing the world, and that I have to try to understand as well as possible the dynamics of our contemporary society. But what really counts is that all this information, knowledge, and insight allow me to speak more clearly and unambiguously your truthful word. Do not allow evil powers to seduce me with the complexities of the world's problems, but give me the strength to think clearly, speak freely and act boldly in your service. Give me the courage to show the dove in a world so full of serpents. Amen.

Sunday, July 15

Dear Lord, you instructed your disciples to take nothing on their journey except a staff, and to stay in the houses of those to whom they came to preach your word. In this state of physical weakness and dependency, they manifested your power and strength. They called people to repentance, cast out devils, anointed and cured many who were sick.

As long as I am still carrying around with me heavy baggage of whatever kind—physical, mental, emotional —and as long as I am still concerned with my own projects and plans, how can I expect to be a real witness to you and a healer of others?

Help me, O Lord, to detach myself more and more from all that prevents you from touching the lives of suffering men, women, and children through me. Show me the way to be poor, so that your richness can become visible, and the way to be weak, so that your strength can become manifest. Amen.

Wednesday, July 18

Dear Lord, no one knows the Father in heaven except you and those to whom you choose to reveal him. How pretentious and faithless it is to want to know God through study, spiritual discussion, or good works. All the books I have read, classes I have attended and retreats I have made cannot give me any true knowledge of God. Only you can reveal him to me. Knowing God, your Father, is indeed the greatest gift you give.

To whom do you choose to give this knowledge? To the learned and clever? No, to mere children, to those who hardly think about themselves but who are open to receive gifts which they themselves cannot understand or imagine.

Will you choose me, too? I often wonder if my knowledge about God has not become my greatest stumbling block to my knowledge of God. But you, O Lord, can open any door and walk through any wall. You can find in me the child who always desires to receive the knowledge of your loving Father. Come, Lord Jesus, and choose me. Amen.

Thursday, July 19

Dear Lord, you say, "Shoulder my yoke and learn from me, for I am gentle and humble in heart." These words stayed with me today because I realized how often I complain about my yoke and hear others complain about theirs. So often I consider life and its many tasks and concerns burdensome, and then it does not take much to become pessimistic or depressed, to ask for attention to my "unique" problem, and to spend much time and energy in expressing annoyance and irritation.

You do not say, "I will take your burden away," but, "I invite you to take on my burden!" Your burden is a real burden. It is the burden of all human sin and failings. You carried that burden and died under its weight. Thus you made it into a light burden.

O Lord, turn my attention from the false burden to the real burden, and let me carry your burden in union with you. I know that only then will I be able to overcome the temptations of bitterness and resentfulness, and live joyfully and gratefully in your service.

Let me better understand your words, "My yoke is easy and my burden light." Amen.

Monday, July 23

Dear Lord, do I want to see signs from you as the Pharisees did? I certainly do not desire miraculous cures or great solar phenomena, but I often find myself hoping that you will touch my own and my friends' hearts in a very distinctive way. I often desire an inner feeling of peace, tranquillity, and sweetness in which your love and goodness can be tasted.

But you, O Lord, ask me to accept the sign of Jonas, the sign of your death and resurrection. You want me to recognize your presence not so much in unusual outer or inner events, but in the painful experience of living in the belly of the sea monster. You do not take your friends out of this world but want them to taste its bitterness with you so that by sharing in your death they can share also in your resurrection.

I pray that I can be faithful to you with no other sign to rely upon than the sign of Jonas. You yourself gave me that sign, and that should be enough.

In you, O Lord, I put my hope. Amen.

Wednesday, July 25
Feast of the Apostle James

Dear Lord, your disciple James longed for a special place in your kingdom, a place close to you. You had a special affection for him; you took him with you when you entered the house of Jairus to heal his daughter and when you went up to Mount Tabor to pray. But you made it clear that friendship with you includes suffering with you. When you asked him if he could drink the cup of suffering, he said yes with the same ambition with which he desired a special place in your kingdom.

You loved this young, zealous man whose main desire was to be with you at all times and in all places. You told him and all your disciples that service, not power, was the standard in your kingdom, and slowly you changed his heart from one set on influence into one searching for the deepest place. He responded, followed you, and drank the same cup you drank. He became one of the first apostles to die for you.

O Lord, convert my heart as you converted the heart of your disciple James. Amen.

Dear Lord, how often have the worries of the world and the attraction of wealth choked your word! For your word to grow deep roots and to yield a rich harvest, it needs a free, open, and untroubled heart. I know, Lord, that your word has power, that it can transform heart and mind and can become so strong that it speaks as if by itself. But how can your word be effective when it is received by a thorny heart, a heart constantly and scrupulously reflecting on what happened yesterday and anxiously anticipating what will happen tomorrow, a heart perverted by guilt, jealousy, envy, and lust, a heart always restless and in turmoil? It is no surprise that such a heart prevents your word from bearing fruit.

O Lord, give me a heart that can receive your word the way good soil receives the falling seed, and let your word produce new life and new love in the midst of this barren world. Amen.

Dear Lord, even when you wanted to be alone with your friends, a large crowd kept following you to hear your word and to feel your healing touch. Moved by their need for a shepherd, you taught them and cured their sick. And when evening came and you noticed their weariness and hunger, you made them sit down on the grass and gave them an abundance of bread and fish so that they would be strong enough to return home safely.

What strikes me, Lord, is that those who follow you without worrying about food and rest receive all they need. Your response to the tempting devil, "Man does not live by bread alone, but on every word that comes from the mouth of God," comes back to mind in this event at the lakeside. Those who hunger for your word also receive enough bread to eat. You indeed care for those who have taken the risk to follow you to lonely places.

O Lord, never let my desire for food or shelter take preference over my desire to hear your word and be healed by your touch. I want to follow you, and trust that you will indeed give me what I need when I need it.

Deepen and strengthen my trust. Amen.

Thursday, August 2

Dear Lord, it seems as if many pains and struggles are being brought to my attention this week. Car accidents, serious illnesses, death, depression, loss of faith, inability to pray, feeling of impotence, and many other events and experiences cry out to you for healing, hope, faith, courage, and strength. O Lord, be with your people; do not leave them in fear and despair, but let them know that you are a faithful God who has made a New Covenant with them and will not go back on your word of love.

Most of all, O Lord, I pray that you help all who suffer to look to you who have carried all the sufferings of the world and have died to bring new life. May those who are in agony and pain see in your cross a sign of hope, and may they catch a glimpse of the mystery that they can make up all that has still to be undergone by you for the sake of your body, the Church. Help us to see that in our suffering we can indeed become intimately connected to your ongoing work of salvation.

O Lord, show all who are in pain your boundless love and mercy. Amen.

Sunday, August 5

Dear Lord, you are the Word of God through whom all creation came into being: rivers and trees, mountains and valleys, birds and horses, wheat and corn, sun and stars, rain and thunder, wind and storm, and above all, people—male and female, young and old, black and white, brown and red, farmers and teachers, monks and businessmen. You, O Lord, can be found in all your creation because it all came into being through the Word of your almighty Father, who spoke the creation into existence and saw that it was good.

I thank you for the beauty of all that is, and I praise you for the artists, painters, sculptors, musicians, dancers, and writers who, by their talents, open my eyes to the splendor of your divine presence in the universe.

Glory to you, O Lord, and to the Father Almighty, maker of heaven and earth. Amen.

Dear Lord, my stay at the Abbey is coming to an end, and in a few days I will no longer have the support of the regular hours of communal prayer, of the silence of the house, and of the loving care of this beautiful brotherhood. I have to move to a busier place to teach, preach, and counsel because it is to that active task that you have called me. But I pray that I will keep you in the center of my thoughts, words, and actions. I pray that your presence, which I have sensed so strongly here, will also guide my life at the university, but most of all I pray that I will keep taking the time to be with you and you alone.

Let the knowledge of your love fill my heart and mind so that I can witness to you freely, openly, and courageously, and bring your peace and your joy to the many who are searching—knowingly or unknowingly—for you. Amen.

Tuesday, August 14

Dear Lord, my heart is filled with gratitude for the time you have given me here at the Abbey of the Genesee. Perhaps my prayer has not been as deep and intimate as I wanted. My mind has often been preoccupied with small worries and petty concerns. But when I look back at this time, I realize that you have given me a real spiritual home. You have given me brothers who consider me one of them and who will care for me wherever I go. I now know that I can always return and be accepted, that I can always ask for prayers, and that I can always count on the strong spiritual support of my brothers here.

I thank you, Lord, for this invaluable grace. I pray that I may live my life as a teacher worthy of this gift, that I may remain faithful to the spirit of this brother-hood, and that I will be able to share the new strength I now experience with all to whom you send me.

O Lord, reveal your abundant blessings to all the brothers who have shown me so clearly the reality of your love. Amen.

EPILOGUE

The prayers in this book were the result of an experiment, an experiment in writing to the Lord. When I look back at my six months of writing prayers I recognize that these prayers hide more than they reveal. They reveal a fearful heart, a cry for mercy, rays of hope, the power of the Spirit, the needs of the world, and finally gratitude. They even reveal a movement from a self-preoccupied introspection to the beginning of an inner freedom that offers space for the pains of others and responds to grace with gratitude. But I have come to realize that what remains hidden is *prayer*.

Rereading these prayers, a year after I wrote them, I now see that my words are no more than the walls that surround a silent place. These prayers are only the context for prayer. If anything has become clear, it is that I cannot pray, but that the Spirit of God prays in me. This divine prayer cannot be expressed in words, it dwells in the silence before, between and beyond the words of a searching heart. Prayer is the breathing of God's Spirit in us. Prayer is the cry of the Spirit, "Abba, Father," coming from the innermost depths of our being. Prayer is the divine life in us, a life of which we are only dimly aware and which transcends the capacities of all our senses. Thus I must say that these prayers hide the prayer of God, which can never be printed in a book.

The mystery of life is that the Lord of life cannot be known except in and through the act of living. Without the concrete and specific involvements of daily life we cannot come to know the loving presence of him who holds us in the palm of his hand. Our limited acts of love reveal to us his unlimited love. Our small gestures of care reveal his boundless care. Our fearful and hesitant words reveal his fearless and guiding Word. It is indeed through our broken, vulnerable, mortal ways of being that the healing power of the eternal God becomes visible to us. Therefore, we are called each day to present to our Lord the whole of our lives—our joys as well as sorrows, our successes as well as failures, our hopes as well as fears. We are called to do so with our limited means, our stuttering words and halting expressions. In this way, we will come to know in mind and heart the unceasing prayer of God's Spirit in us. Our many prayers are in fact confessions of our inability to pray. But they are confessions that enable us to perceive the merciful presence of God. Our prayers are as unique as our individual lives. The prayers in this book are those of one human being. May there be many more prayers by many more people so that the everlasting prayer of God, which cannot be expressed in words, will continue to make itself known.